*An eighteenth-century Dutch tile with an ornate purple border and showing a hunter and a woman returning home accompanied by two dogs.*

# DELFTWARE TILES

### Hans van Lemmen

2

Published in 2011 by Shire Publications Ltd,
Midland House, West Way, Botley, Oxford, OX2 0PH UK.
(Website: www.shirebooks.co.uk)

British Library Cataloguing in Publication Data:
Lemmen, Hans van
Delftware tiles. – 2nd ed. – (Shire Library; 179)
1. Delftware – History
2. Tiles – History
I. Title
738.3'7
ISBN 0 74780 611 X.

*Cover: Late-nineteenth-century 15 cm Dutch delftware tiles made by J. van Hulst, Harlingen, Friesland, Netherlands.*

ACKNOWLEDGEMENTS
The following people and institutions have been of assistance in the production of this book.
Thanks to Dr Richard Tyler for reading and commenting on the manuscript, and to Chris
Blanchett, Evert van Gelder, Roger Hensman and Charles Krafft for permission to use
photographs of tiles from their collections. Also special thanks to Charles Allen, Stephen
Cocker, Bobby Jones and Joop van der Werf, who as professional tilemakers have
demonstrated delftware tile-production techniques to the author. Photographs from public
collections are acknowledged as follows: National Museum and Art Galleries on Merseyside,
page 23; Nederlands Openlucht Museum, Arnhem, page 31; Nederlands Tegelmuseum,
Otterlo, pages 4 (bottom), 5 (bottom), 12 (bottom), 13 (bottom), 14 (all), 15 (bottom), 16
(both), 17 (both), 18 (top two, centre, bottom left), 19 (both), 21 (bottom), 22 (top), 32
(top), 35 (top two); Royal Scottish Museum, Edinburgh, page 32 (bottom).

Printed in China through Worldprint Ltd.

# CONTENTS

*A fireplace at Aston Hall, Birmingham, decorated with English delftware tiles depicting Chinese figures set within fish-roe borders and Michaelmas daisy corners; Liverpool or Bristol, 1750–75.*

*A Dutch tile of c.1625–50 showing a tulip, and with large ox-head corner motifs.*

# INTRODUCTION

Delftware pottery and tiles were in great demand during the seventeenth and eighteenth centuries. The term 'delftware' is generally used to indicate functional or decorative earthenware pottery covered with an opaque white tin glaze on which decorations have been painted in blue or other colours. The term is derived from the Dutch town of Delft, where from the seventeenth century many potteries produced hand-painted tin-glazed pottery of high quality that was exported all over the world. The potteries in Delft produced tiles alongside their other wares but tiles were not a major product. Most Dutch tiles were manufactured in such places as Rotterdam, Amsterdam, Utrecht and

*A mid-seventeenth-century Dutch tile showing a camel, and with ox-head corner motifs.*

*An English delftware tile showing a sailing boat flying the English ensign, and with barred ox-head corner motifs; London, 1720–50.*

Gouda, and in the north of the country in Harlingen and Makkum, where tiles were often the main line of business. Delftware was also made in Britain, at first by Flemish and Dutch potters who had settled mainly in London at the end of the sixteenth century and in the seventeenth. However, no specialist delftware tile factories were ever established in Britain and tiles were only one aspect of their output.

Delftware tiles form a special category within the history of delftware pottery. Since they were mainly applied to walls and fireplaces, they belong to the history of architectural ceramics. Their prime purpose was functional but the many scenes and decorations painted on them have made them a fascinating field of study, which is one reason why they are now eagerly collected or carefully preserved *in situ*.

*A late-nineteenth-century Dutch polychrome landscape tile. The ornate border has a red powdered ground.*

# MAKING DELFTWARE TILES

The basic methods of making and decorating delftware tiles are as follows. Prepared clay is rolled into flat slabs from which rough squares are cut. A rough square is then placed between two wooden slats and rolled flat and even. An exact square is now cut with the aid of a square wooden template and left to dry. Another method is to place a roughly cut square of clay in a wooden or iron frame and to level the clay within the square frame. When the frame is lifted away a perfectly formed square tile is left. After a period of drying the tiles have to be rolled and flattened again and if they lose their shape they may have to be trimmed square again. After further drying, the tile is fired for the first time at a temperature around 950–1000°C. After firing, the biscuit tiles are checked and sorted and are ready to be glazed.

The white tin glaze is applied to one side of the tile only by dipping it into a tub or bucket filled with liquid glaze. The biscuit will absorb the water rapidly, leaving a thin, powder-like layer of white tin glaze on the surface of the tile. When completely dry, the tile is ready for decorating. The painter places a transfer pricked with a particular design or pattern (called *spons* in Dutch) on the unfired white glaze and pounces charcoal through the holes pricked in the transfer. When this is removed, a faint outline of the design can be seen. The painter then outlines the design (a process called *trek* in Dutch) with a colour such as cobalt blue, which is pigment ground fine and mixed with water. After the design has been delineated, the various tints and shades are added. Until the middle of the seventeenth century it was customary for Dutch tiles to be given an extra coat of clear transparent glaze (called *kwaart* in Dutch) to add extra brilliance to the surface of the tile.

*Cutting a tile with the aid of a square wooden template.*

*A fired biscuit tile ready to be dipped into tin glaze.*

*A biscuit tile is dipped into the tin glaze.*

*A dipped tile covered with a thin, even layer of white tin glaze.*

A pin-pricked design, called 'spons' in Dutch, with an ornate octagonal border pattern.

A pin-pricked design with a landscape.

A tile with a charcoal imprint left by the pin-pricked design and used as a guide by the painter.

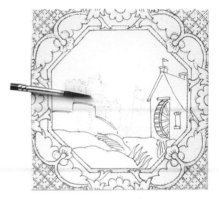

A tile with the outlines of the charcoal design partially painted in. The process of tracing the outline of the design is called 'trek' in Dutch.

A tile with all the tints and shades added in, ready to be fired. The dull grey and black colours will be transformed into a bright blue during the firing.

The fired tile showing the landscape and decorative border in all its vivid blue colouring.

*The delftware tile-painter Bobby Jones at work in his studio at Orleton Manor, Orleton, near Ludlow, Shropshire.*

After the tile has been painted it is fired a second time at about 1000°C, during which the white powder-like glaze becomes opaque and glassy. The blue or other high-temperature pigment sinks into the glaze and fuses permanently with it. On certain special tiles on-glaze enamels were used. They were painted on after the tin-glaze firing and were fixed to the glaze during a special third firing in a muffle kiln at a lower temperature, between 600 and 800°C. Although the basic procedures outlined here seem simple, much experience and skill are needed to complete each phase satisfactorily. The success of the delftware trade depended (and still does) on the expertise being passed on from master to apprentice.

# FLEMISH ORIGINS

The technique of making tin-glazed pottery and tiles was introduced to the Low Countries (modern Belgium and the Netherlands) by Italian maiolica potters at the beginning of the sixteenth century. Antwerp in Flanders, now part of Belgium, became one of the main centres of this trade and among the Italian potters who established workshops there was Guido di Savino from Castel Durante. He changed his name to the more Flemish-sounding Andries when he married a local woman from Antwerp in 1512. Guido Andries began to manufacture maiolica pottery and tiles by covering already fired clay pots, plates and tiles with white tin glaze and painting decorations on them in blue, yellow, orange and green. This strikingly colourful maiolica pottery soon became very popular and tiles made by this technique were used as floor tiles. It seems that maiolica floor tiles made in Antwerp were also exported to England since there is a remarkably early example at The Vyne, Sherborne St John, Hampshire. The Vyne is a red-brick Tudor house built between 1500 and 1520 for William Sandys, Lord Chamberlain under Henry VIII. The chapel in the house has a floor covered with maiolica tiles, some of which have Flemish inscriptions, and these may well have been made in the workshop of Guido Andries in Antwerp.

Guido Andries passed on his trade to his many sons and the business became a well-established family concern. At that time Spain ruled the

Low Countries but, when the Dutch demanded independence, war broke out between Spain and the Netherlands. Antwerp was at the centre of the hostilities and was sacked a number of times. Merchants, artists and craftsmen left the city for safer places in the north. Maiolica potters also left Antwerp and among them were Joris Andries, who settled in Middelburg, Zeeland, in 1564, Adriaen Bogaert, who went to Haarlem in about 1565, and Carstiaen van den Abeele, who set up a workshop in Amsterdam in 1584. Jasper Andries and Jacob Jansen came to England and settled in Norwich in 1567. This is how the technique of making maiolica pottery and tiles spread to the Netherlands and England.

*Early-sixteenth-century maiolica floor tiles in the chapel at The Vyne, Sherborne St John, Hampshire. It is possible that they were made in the workshop of Guido di Savino (Guido Andries) in Antwerp. The tile with the jester bears the inscription SOTGE, which is a Flemish word for 'fool'.*

# EARLY DUTCH DELFTWARE TILES

Floor tiles had been made in the Netherlands since the Middle Ages, but they were made from red-firing clay covered with a thin coat of transparent lead glaze. Sometimes patterns of white clay were laid into the red tile body. When laid on the floor these tiles could create strong decorative effects, but they could not match the colourfully painted maiolica tiles introduced by potters from Antwerp. Despite the attractive qualities of maiolica tiles, they were not very suitable for walking on. The painted decorations wore quickly and the thrifty Dutch soon began to use tiles on walls, where they would last longer and proved effective against damp and dirt. Canals intersect many towns in the Netherlands and many houses stand with their foundations in water, where lack of proper insulation caused constant damp problems. Tiles were therefore used in cellars, but also in kitchens, in fireplaces and as wall skirting closing the gap between the floor and the wall. Their glass-like, glazed surfaces were easily cleaned, and their patterns and pictures introduced a decorative element. Paintings by seventeenth-century artists such as Vermeer and De Hoogh show how tiles were used in Dutch interiors.

At the beginning of the seventeenth century the Netherlands had emerged as an independent nation free of Spanish domination and its ports and worldwide sea trade brought considerable prosperity. Towns expanded and many new houses were built. The wealth created was more evenly distributed among the Dutch population than in other European countries. A large and broadly based middle class emerged who could afford to spend money on such luxuries as tiles for their homes. Millions of tiles were produced to keep pace with increased demand.

*A panel of early-seventeenth-century Dutch tiles showing flowerpots. The large corner motifs have been painted in the 'reserving' technique and where four corner motifs meet they form a decorative unit similar in size to the central motif of each tile.*

An early-seventeenth-century Dutch tile with a large blue-and-white corner motif painted in the 'reserving' technique. Four tiles are needed to complete the whole design.

An early-seventeenth-century Dutch tile showing an elephant set within a diamond frame with large corner motifs executed in the reserving technique.

The tiles produced at the end of the sixteenth century were not very different from the Antwerp maiolica tiles. Square pieces of pink-firing clay were covered with white tin glaze and received polychrome decorations that ran over more than one tile. Around 1600, when the Dutch wall tile became an important functional and decorative wall cladding, different designs were introduced. Animals, flowerpots and

*An early-seventeenth-century Dutch tile made in Rotterdam and depicting a Roman auxiliary soldier. The four pinholes in the corners are clearly visible.*

*A Dutch tile of 1625–50 with the portrait of a lady.*

designs with grapes and pomegranates became popular as central motifs within a diamond-shaped or circular border on single tiles. The corners of each tile were filled with stylised leaf motifs executed in the so-called 'reserving technique'. When put together on the wall, the corner motifs met and formed large decorative units almost equal in size to the central figurative designs.

*A Dutch tile of 1625–50 with ox-head corner motifs and depicting a bird (possibly a finch).*

*A Dutch tile of 1625–50 depicting a stork.*

*A Dutch tile of 1640–70 showing a winged cherub.*

*A Dutch tile of 1625–50 with Chinese meander corner motifs and a central scene depicting a bird, an insect and flowers, and showing the influence of designs on Chinese porcelain.*

A decisive change in the decoration of early-seventeenth-century Dutch tiles occurred when the United Dutch East India Company, founded in 1602, began to import blue-and-white Chinese porcelain. The craze for Ming porcelain that followed had an adverse effect on local manufacturers of maiolica pottery, although tiles were not directly affected as no tiles were imported from China. To maintain their hold on the market, Dutch potters began to imitate Chinese porcelain. Although they could not make actual porcelain, by making their earthenware thinner and more delicate and painting blue-and-white Chinese motifs on the white tin glaze, they produced a type of pottery almost indistinguishable from real porcelain. Tiles followed suit and around 1620 Dutch tiles with blue-and-white Chinese patterns appeared on the market.

*A Dutch tile of 1625–50 with Chinese meander corner motifs and a central scene depicting a dog.*

The fashion for Chinese designs on tiles did not last long and soon the interest of the Dutch tile-painter turned to scenes taken from daily life. Pictures of men and women in Dutch costumes, of trades and occupations, soldiers, portraits and animals began to appear on tiles mostly painted in blue embellished with all kinds of different corner motifs. By the middle of the seventeenth century the range of subject matter had been extended with sea-creatures, cupids and soldiers on horseback, while in the second half of the seventeenth century landscapes, children's games and biblical scenes appeared. At this time corner motifs became smaller and sometimes were omitted altogether.

*A Dutch tile of 1630–50 with fleur-de-lis corner motifs and showing a well-dressed fashionable couple.*

*A Dutch tile of 1620–50 with fleur-de-lis corner motifs and depicting either a donkey or a mule set between two balusters.*

A Dutch tile of 1625–50 with ox-head corner motifs and depicting a shoemaker sitting on a chair.

A panel of nine Dutch tiles depicting a variety of animals and with ox-head corner motifs, c.1650.

Above left: *A mid-seventeenth-century tile with ox-head corner motifs and showing a large merchant ship with billowing sails.*

Above right: *A very rare Dutch tile with a polychrome landscape painted on blue tin glaze, 1650–1700.*

Left: *A Dutch tile with a portrait of Enno Ludwig of Ostfriesland, 1650–75.*

Below left: *A Dutch tile of the middle of the seventeenth century with ox-head corner motifs and depicting a merman holding a torch and an eel.*

Below right: *In the period 1650–1700 tilemakers made their production processes more cost-effective by making their tiles thinner and the painted pictures much simpler, like this tile with a small winged cherub blowing a trumpet and small spider's head corner motifs.*

*A Dutch landscape tile with fleur-de-lis corner motifs and a purple powdered border, c.1700.*

Engravings often served as examples for tiles, and prints of soldiers by Jacob van Gheyn and prints with biblical scenes by Pieter Schut were often copied.

Although most Dutch tiles were produced elsewhere in the Netherlands, the tiles made in Delft were often of outstanding quality. Potters in Delft had become very successful in imitating various forms of Chinese as well as Japanese polychrome porcelain and in some instances this was transferred to tiles. Some exquisite tile panels that combine in-glaze pigments such as blue and purple with on-glaze enamels like red, yellow and gold have been attributed to De Roos (The Rose) factory in Delft. The Grieksche A (Greek A) factory in Delft was awarded prestigious commissions from King William III and his wife Queen Mary II. When Hampton Court, near London, was refurbished between 1689 and 1694, the Grieksche A was asked to make tiles and pottery for the dairy according to designs by the famous French émigré designer Daniel Marot.

*A tile panel depicting a seascape, painted by Cornelis Boumeester in Rotterdam, c.1700. The barrel floating in the sea at the bottom left has the painter's initials CBM.*

*Three sumptuous Dutch tile panels with flower bouquets in vases executed in an elaborate array of colours, in the kitchen of the Amalienburg pavilion at Schloss Nymphenburg in Munich, Germany. Made in either Delft or Rotterdam c.1735.*

Royal commissions also came from Germany and France. Factories in Rotterdam made the tiles used in various buildings at Schloss Nymphenburg near Munich built for the Elector Max Emanuel at the beginning of the eighteenth century. Tiles made in Rotterdam at this time were also used at Schloss Augustusburg and the Jagdschloss Falkenlust at Brühl near Cologne, built for the Elector Clemens August. The grand staircase in the Jagdschloss at Brühl is decorated with specially designed tiles showing hunting scenes made by the Bloempot factory of Jan Aalmis in Rotterdam. Such commissions helped to spread the fame of Dutch tiles throughout Europe. The tile-painter Cornelis Boumeester (1652–1733) was also active in Rotterdam and worked at the tile factory at

*Tiles at Jagdschloss Falkenlust in Brühl near Cologne, built between 1729 and 1737, showing hunting scenes with falcons chasing herons. The tiles were made at the Bloempot factory of Jan Aalmis in Rotterdam.*

*Two eighteenth-century tile panels with flower bouquets in a fireplace in John Knox's House, Edinburgh. They were made in the Bloempot factory of Jan Aalmis in Rotterdam. The flower pieces are based on prints by the Dutch artist Carl Allard (1648–1709).*

the Delftse Vaart. He specialised in painting large harbour scenes, seascapes and sea battles, all executed in tones of blue. His work was in great demand and his panels were exported abroad. Examples are the Boumeester panels with seascapes at Château de Rambouillet near Paris, built for the Comte de Toulouse about 1730.

While at the end of the seventeenth century and the beginning of the eighteenth century the export market for Dutch tiles had been extended with high profile commissions from abroad, the home market had undergone changes, which affected the production of tiles. Towards the end of the seventeenth century the demand for tiles in urban areas declined. Changes in fireplace design were one cause, but at the same time the demand for decorative tiles in rural areas rose. Well-to-do

*An eighteenth-century tile made in Delft showing a flower basket set in a circular border in imitation of Chinese and Japanese porcelain. Executed in on-glaze enamel colours and gold.*

*Dutch eighteenth-century biblical tiles at the Dutch Tile Museum (Nederlands Tegelmuseum) in Otterlo. The central tile depicts an Old Testament scene with Samson pulling down the pillars to which he had been chained.*

farmers installed large fireplaces decorated with tiles and occasionally whole rooms were lined with them. Landscape tiles and tiles with biblical scenes were very popular, but there was also an increased use of tiles with purely decorative patterns, mostly painted in blue or purple. Next to blue, purple (derived from manganese oxide) became an increasingly important colour in eighteenth-century tile decoration. The influence of French decorative design is noticeable on the many tiles with rococo scrolls or with the elaborate borders used for many landscape tiles.

The late eighteenth century was a difficult time for the Dutch tile industry. By then tiles were manufactured in only a few places, the main ones being Rotterdam, Utrecht, Makkum and Harlingen. The rising fashion for wallpaper was damaging the industry and so was Napoleon's conquest of the Netherlands, which had an adverse effect on trade and exports. The increasing output of Staffordshire tableware pioneered by Josiah Wedgwood was felt by the whole Dutch tin-glazed earthenware industry. Many factories had to close and relatively few survived into the nineteenth century.

*An eighteenth-century Dutch tile painted in dark purple and depicting a Chinaman.*

An English delftware tile made in London c.1680, inscribed 'The Plot first hatcht at Rome by the Pope and Cardinalls &ct'. This is from a series of tiles based on contemporary playing cards illustrating the so-called 'Popish Plot', a conspiracy in 1678 to kill Charles II.

# ENGLISH DELFTWARE TILES

The technique of making tin-glazed ware was brought to Britain by Flemish and Dutch potters such as Jasper Andries and Jacob Jansen, who had settled in Norwich in 1567. In 1570 they both went to London to petition Queen Elizabeth I for permission to set up a pottery business for 'the Makinge of Galley pavinge tiles and Vessels for potycaries'. The petition was not successful and Andries moved back to Norwich, but Jansen stayed in London, where in 1571 he is recorded as 'Pot-maker'.

A Dutch potter by the name of Christian Wilhelm was active in Southwark in the first quarter of the seventeenth century, while in 1676 the Dutch potter Jan Aries van Hamme moved from Delft to Lambeth in London for 'making Tiles and Porcelain and other earthen wares after the way practised in Holland'. Compared to production in the Netherlands at that time, the output of delftware tiles in England was very small and many tiles had to be imported from the Netherlands despite an import ban imposed on Dutch delftware in 1672.

The British delftware tile industry reached a peak of production during the eighteenth century. The main centres were London, Bristol and Liverpool and some tiles were also produced at the Delftfield factory in Glasgow. Until about 1750 many English delftware tiles were closely based on Dutch examples, particularly those made in London. Factories in Lambeth produced single tiles depicting flower vases, landscapes, pastoral scenes, ships and biblical subjects. The Dutch

Above left: *An English delftware tile with barred ox-head corner motifs and a scene depicting the flagellation of Christ; London, 1725–50.*

Above right: *An English delftware tile with barred ox-head corner motifs and a scene depicting the Ascension of Christ; London, 1725–50.*

Below left: *An English delftware tile with carnation corner motifs and a sailing ship set within an octagonal border with a blue powdered ground; London, 1725–50.*

Below right: *An English delftware tile with carnation corner motifs and a landscape with a fisherman set within an octagonal border with a purple powdered ground; London, c.1725–50.*

*Detail of the tiles in the 'Blue Loo' at Chatham Historic Dockyard, Kent, showing English delftware tiles with landscapes and barred ox-head corner motifs; London, c.1760–90.*

influence is perhaps not surprising, given the many Dutch potters who had settled in London in the seventeenth century. The uses made of tiles in the Netherlands were more varied than in Britain, where they were mainly used in fireplaces or sometimes for tiled alcoves with wash-basins. Occasionally English delftware tiles were also used as signs for eighteenth-century inns or coffee-houses.

The difference between Dutch and English tiles can be detected from the way they are painted, in the composition of the tin glaze and in the make-up of the clay body. Dutch tiles are generally painted in a more assured manner and with greater deftness. The tin glaze of Dutch tiles is usually whiter because it contains more tin oxide, although this is liable to craze. English tin glaze is often somewhat bluish and much glossier and smoother than Dutch glaze and it does not craze easily. On English tiles the blue decorations have sometimes sunk below the level of the glaze, creating perceptible hollows. This is a particular

*A rare English delftware tile with a marbled border and 'cracked ice' corner motifs, and with a bird in the centre; London, 1750–75.*

*An English delftware tile with cherub corner motifs and an Old Testament scene showing the prophet Elijah fed by ravens; London or Bristol, 1725–50.*

feature of some Liverpool tiles. The clay body of English tiles tends to be harder and denser than that of the Dutch, which is softer with a more sandy texture. This made Dutch tiles easier to trim and for that reason it seems builders preferred Dutch tiles to English ones. Nail holes left on the front of the tile as part of the cutting and trimming process are very common on Dutch tiles, but less common on English tiles, which sometimes have nail holes on the back.

After 1750 English delftware tiles became less dependent on Dutch examples and the central designs, borders and corner motifs began to show greater originality. This can be seen in tiles made in Liverpool,

*An English delftware tile with flower-head corner motifs and the Old Testament scene of Elijah leaving Elisha in a chariot of fire; Bristol, 1725–50.*

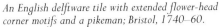
*An English delftware tile with extended flower-head corner motifs and a pikeman; Bristol, 1740–60.*

Below: *An English delftware tile with a bianco-sopara-bianco border and a polychrome flower basket; Bristol, 1760–75.*

where, in addition to the standard blue and purple, colours such as green, yellow and red were introduced. Polychrome Liverpool tiles with birds and 'chinoiserie' figures are now highly prized. The potters in Bristol also introduced colour, but they are now better known for the development of *bianco-sopara-bianco* (white-on-white) borders on tiles. This is a particular English feature never found on Dutch delftware tiles.

In 1756 another unusual development took place in Liverpool. White glazed but otherwise undecorated delftware tiles were

*An English delftware tile with a bianco-sopara-bianco border and a central floral design; Liverpool, 1760–75.*

*Detail of an English delftware tile depicting skaters on ice, executed with confident brushwork; Liverpool, 1750–75.*

Left: *An English delftware tile with rosette corner motifs and a boatman set within an octagonal border; Liverpool, 1750–75.*

*An English delftware tile with a river scene and unusual cherub corner motifs; Liverpool, 1750–75.*

*A fascinating assortment of mainly eighteenth-century English delftware tiles in a pantry at Shide House, Newport, Isle of Wight. (The tiles are no longer in situ.)*

used for printing experiments by John Sadler. There is an affidavit of 27th July 1756, sworn in front of witnesses, stating that John Sadler and his assistant, Guy Green, printed more than twelve hundred tiles within the space of six hours, many more than any painter could do by hand. The novelty of the technique lay in transferring an image from an engraved copper plate to plain white glazed delftware with the aid of a thin sheet of gelatine (bat printing), although the first experiments were achieved by taking prints from wood blocks. Some of the printed tiles were coloured in by hand with on-glaze enamels, but most of them are without colour and were printed in monochrome black, red and brown. The decorations were fired on to the surface of the tile in a muffle kiln at a low temperature of 600–800°C.

*Two tiles printed by John Sadler in Liverpool. (Left) A print taken from a wood block, with enamel colours added by hand, showing a courting couple, 1756–7. (Right) A print taken from an engraved copper plate depicting the game blind man's buff, 1757–61.*

Above left: *A printed tile by John Sadler of Liverpool depicting Trajan's Column with the Temple of Castor, signed 'J. Sadler Liverpool', 1758–61.*

Above right: *A printed tile probably by Sadler's successor Guy Green in Liverpool, depicting the actress Mrs Yates in the role of Jane Shore, 1777–80.*

Left: *A printed tile, probably by Sadler's successor Guy Green in Liverpool, depicting the Three Graces against a background painted in green enamel, 1770–80.*

The range of subjects on printed delftware tiles is considerable. There are numerous open-air scenes with figures of fashionable society and scenes from rustic life. Other themes are ships, games, fables, biblical scenes, romantic ruins, chinoiserie subjects and classical vases. But perhaps the most interesting of all are the portraits of contemporary actors and actresses of the English theatre. They are usually portrayed in their famous stage roles and each tile often bears the name of the actor or actress and the title of the play.

During the second half of the eighteenth century delftware potters began to experience the competition of industrially produced pottery from Staffordshire made by such men as Josiah Wedgwood and Josiah Spode in highly organised factories. Wedgwood's creamware and Spode's blue-and-white underglaze-printed pottery had driven most traditional delftware pottery makers out of existence by about 1800. A few delftware factories in London survived into the early nineteenth century but by about 1840 they had all closed down.

# LATE DUTCH DELFTWARE TILES

The few remaining delftware factories in the Netherlands had mixed fortunes from the late eighteenth century onwards. In Rotterdam, the famous De Bloempot factory was owned by three different families: it belonged to the Aalmis family until 1788, when it was sold to Laurens Verwijk; then in 1842 it was bought by Willem van Traa, who closed it down in 1852. At the town of Delfshaven, near Rotterdam, F. J. Kleyn, an ex-employee of the Bloempot factory, set up his own small tilery in 1851 and remained in business until 1866. He called his firm 'Piet Hein' after a famous Dutch admiral of that name, who was born in Delfshaven in 1578. A rare collection of delftware tiles made at the Piet Hein factory survives in the Royal Scottish Museum in Edinburgh, donated by F. J. Kleyn in 1861. A tile-pattern book now known as the Rotterdam Pattern Book was donated by Kleyn to the Rotterdam City Archive in 1876, where it can still be seen today. An interesting tile legacy of this small and short-lived factory has therefore survived.

*The interior of a nineteenth-century Dutch farmhouse at the Open Air Museum (Nederlands Openlucht Museum) in Arnhem, Netherlands, with tiles in the fireplace and on the walls.*

A corner of the Dutch Tile Museum in Otterlo with a cast-iron stove set against a wall decorated with late-nineteenth-century flowerpot tiles.

The tile factories in Friesland generally fared better. The already well-established factory of Tichelaar in Makkum produced many tiles throughout the nineteenth and twentieth centuries and is one of the few places in the Netherlands where authentic hand-painted delftware tiles are still being made. Van Hulst in Harlingen became a major tile manufacturer in 1850, after taking over an existing firm, and was in business until 1933. Also in Harlingen was the firm of Tjallingii, which produced tiles between 1781 and 1910. All the Friesian firms supplied tiles to the large rural areas in the northern Netherlands, where traditional Dutch tiles were still in demand. But they also exported considerable quantities to northern Germany, Denmark and Britain.

A promotional tile for F. J. Kleyn's Piet Hein factory in Delfshaven, 1851–66.

*A tile panel on the façade of one of the buildings of the Tichelaar factory painted by Willem ten Zweege and dating from 1895. It shows a view of the Tichelaar factory in Makkum, situated alongside the Grote Zijlroede waterway. Boat transport was essential for bringing raw materials to the factory and taking away the finished products.*

In the early twentieth century Martin van Straaten, a Dutchman who had settled in London, where he ran a tile-import business, often handled their exports to Britain. His name can be found in the company records of both van Hulst and Tichelaar. A number of hand-drawn and printed catalogues of the firms of Tichelaar, van Hulst and Tjallingii have survived and they show a fascinating range of single tile designs as well as tile panels. There are even Arts and Crafts and Art Nouveau tile designs among the traditional Dutch designs, which shows that the Friesian manufacturers tuned in to new design fashions when required.

*A late-nineteenth-century polychrome Dutch tile depicting a peony, made by van Hulst in Harlingen. This tile was made for export to England in a special 15 by 15 cm format. The design shows the influence of the Arts and Crafts movement and is probably based on a floral pattern by the English artist Lewis Day.*

*A page from a printed catalogue of the firm J. van Hulst in Harlingen showing a range of patterned tiles and landscape tiles, c.1895. The landscape tiles have an interesting variety of different borders.*

Left: *A late-nineteenth-century polychrome Dutch landscape tile made by van Hulst in Harlingen in a 15 by 15 cm format.*

*A Dutch landscape tile made by van Hulst in Harlingen, c.1900. The colour green is unusual and tiles like this were exported to Britain.*

*Two late-nineteenth-century Dutch tile panels made in Utrecht, one showing a man with a horse, the other a woman with a cow.*

In Utrecht there was even a small revival of tile production. The brothers Ravesteijn began the production of wall tiles in 1845, while J. Schillemans established a tile factory in 1856. They mainly supplied the town of Utrecht and the rural areas around it. Tiles were used not only in interior locations but also on the façades of houses, where they were used as decorative features above doors and windows and

*A recessed window arch on the façade of a late-nineteenth-century house on the Vleutenseweg in Utrecht. The biblical tiles with straight ox-head corner motifs show a range of scenes from the Old and New Testaments. It is a rare example of biblical tiles on the exterior of a house.*

*A Dutch tile of c.1885 with fleur-de-lis corner motifs and showing a smoker sitting on a bench, probably made by J. Schillemans in Utrecht.*

sometimes under the eaves. J. W. Mijnlieff renamed the firm 'Holland' when he took over the Schillemans factory in 1894. Although initially he continued to produce traditional Dutch tiles, new designs derived from the Arts and Crafts and Art Nouveau movements were introduced around 1900, some of which were designed by Jac van den Bosch. The firm of Holland closed down at the end of the First World War.

*Dutch tiles in the porch of a house on the Koninginneweg, Amsterdam, made by the firm of Holland in Utrecht, showing a design called 'Waterkip' ('waterhen') by the designer Jac van den Bosch, c.1900. The influence of the Arts and Crafts movement is clearly noticeable.*

*A tile panel on the exterior of the old Ravesteijn factory in Utrecht. It shows the Roman god Hermes and bears the inscription 'Tegel Fabriek van de Gebr. Ravesteijn 1845' ('Tile factory of the brothers Ravesteijn 1845').*

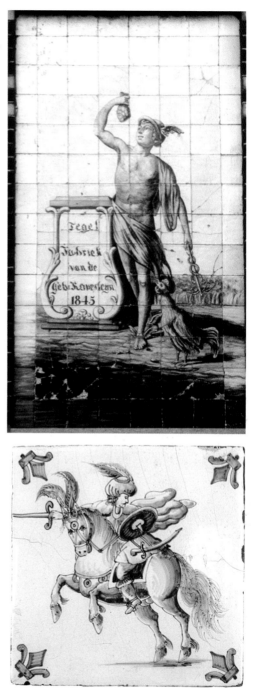

The Ravesteijn factory produced many tiles during the second half of the nineteenth century and even captured a corner of the British tile market, despite the dominance of Victorian industrial tile manufacture. The main reason for this was the Arts and Crafts movement, whose advocates such as William Morris favoured hand-made products over industrially made ones. Already in the 1860s and 1870s Morris & Company in London had imported Dutch tile blanks to be decorated by them in their own workshop. Since their on-glaze decorations were less durable than the in-glaze technique used by the Dutch factories, Morris & Company seem to have franchised the production of certain of their own designs to Ravesteijn and perhaps also to van Hulst in Harlingen. Ravesteijn, however, seem to have been the main supplier as many Morris & Company tile designs appear in their printed catalogues of the late nineteenth and early twentieth centuries, including the well-known 'Daisy' pattern designed

*A Dutch tile with fleur-de-lis corner motifs and a Saracen knight on horseback, probably made by Ravesteijn in Utrecht, c.1900.*

A page from a printed tile catalogue of the firm of Ravesteijn in Utrecht, c.1900. It shows traditional Dutch tile designs and various patterned motifs. Design number 113 is a Morris & Company design called 'Longden', attributed to Philip Webb.

by Morris himself. William Morris may have used middlemen in London such as Charles Marks (of Dutch descent) or his successor Thomas Elsley, who imported tiles from the Netherlands for use in high-quality cast-iron grates, which they had made for a select clientele. Although the standard size of traditional Dutch tiles is

A tile made by Ravesteijn in Utrecht between 1880 and 1900, with a daisy design by William Morris. Such tiles were made for Morris & Company in London in 15 by 15 cm format.

A fireplace at Edes House, Chichester, West Sussex, with a series of late-nineteenth-century animal tiles made by Ravesteijn in Utrecht in a 15 by 15 cm format. The various domestic and exotic animals are based on prints from books of the sixteenth and seventeenth centuries, such as Jonston's 'Historia Naturalis'.

13 by 13 cm, Ravesteijn also produced them in 15 by 15 cm format specifically for the British market. Ravesteijn changed their name to Westraven in 1907 and kept up production throughout the twentieth century. In 1985 they moved away from Utrecht to Groenekan, where they remained until closing down in 1994.

Delft, which was once the prime location in the Netherlands for the manufacture of delftware pottery and tiles, with up to thirty ceramic factories in operation, was reduced

A copper-plate engraving (left) of a deer in Doctor Johannes Jonston's 'Historia Naturalis', published in Frankfurt in 1650, and (above) a late-nineteenth-century Dutch tile based on this print. The tile was made by Ravesteijn in Utrecht in 15 by 15 cm format and fitted in a standard English cast-iron grate.

JOOST THOOFT & LABOUCHERE
DELFT

PLATTEN 15¹/₂ × 15¹/₂ cM. — MUSTER C.

*A page from an early-twentieth-century catalogue showing tiles made by De Porceleyne Fles in Delft. The tiles have traditional Dutch landscape motifs and would have been executed in an underglaze technique.*

to one factory, De Porceleyne Fles ('The Porcelain Bottle'), at the end of the nineteenth century. The firm's main line had always been pottery, but when Joost Thooft bought it in 1876 tile manufacture was introduced alongside the production of pottery. Initially some delftware tiles were made using the traditional in-glaze method but soon the firm switched to the production of blue-and-white tiles painted in an underglaze technique. This meant first painting the design on a white biscuit tile, which would then be covered with a transparent glaze. They produced some traditional Dutch tile designs in this way but copies of paintings by well-known Dutch artists were also manufactured in the form of tile panels painted in blue and white. De Porceleyne Fles expanded further in the twentieth century and is still a major producer of ceramics and tiles today.

*A late-nineteenth-century tile panel executed in an underglaze technique and made by De Porceleyne Fles factory in Delft, showing a winter landscape based on a painting by the Dutch artist Louis Apol (1850–1936). It is in the kitchen of a house in Menston, West Yorkshire.*

*A tile by the Dutch delftware painter Joop van der Werf depicting an Old Testament scene of Jonah and the Whale, with ox-head corner motifs, 2000.*

# PRESENT-DAY DELFTWARE TILE ARTISTS

The tradition of delftware tiles is carried on not only at a few large factories but also by a number of individual tile artists in the Netherlands, Britain and even the United States. One such artist in the Netherlands is Joop van der Werf of Keramiek Klassiek in Zaandam. One of his specialities is the painting of traditional Dutch tiles with biblical scenes for use in fireplaces, often as part of contemporary restoration projects. In Britain Bobby Jones in Orleton near Ludlow, Shropshire, makes authentic tin-glazed delftware tiles but also experiments with new designs and new decoration methods such as screen-printing on tin glaze. Charles Allen of New Castle Delft in

*A tile by the British delftware artist Bobby Jones showing a jockey on a horse, 2000.*

*A panel of nine tiles by the British delftware artist Bobby Jones showing delftware-style landscapes with ox-head corner motifs screen-printed on tin glaze, 2000.*

Above: *A panel of three tiles by the British delftware painter Charles Allen depicting a fish with corners accentuated by ox-head corner motifs, 2000.*

Left: *Charles Allen painting the tiles that make up the fish panel.*

*A tile by the British delftware painter Stephen Cocker. The simple design focuses on different kinds of brushwork accentuated with a simple white line pattern executed in sgraffito, 2000.*

Newcastle upon Tyne produces his own hand-made tiles covered with tin glaze and decorates them in blue-and-white in an idiosyncratic style. Stephen Cocker in Bedale, North Yorkshire, creates modernistic tile designs in which he explores different delftware line and brushwork techniques and, like Charles Allen, works exclusively on his own hand-made and tin-glazed tiles. In the United States Charles Krafft makes tiles at his workshop, the Villa Delirium Delft Works in Seattle, Washington. He often takes typically American subjects, which are painted in blue-and-white set within prominent seventeenth-century Dutch tile borders. Although all these artists work in the delftware tradition, they do not slavishly copy established designs. They are inspired by the rich tradition of delftware and borrow elements from it in conjunction with new ideas and subjects linking the past with the present.

*A panel of two tiles by the American delftware artist Charles Krafft. The scene depicts Dutch Schulz, a notorious gangster of the inter-war period, awaiting the outcome of his trial. The scene is set within large traditional Dutch corner motifs executed in the 'reserving technique', 1997.*

# GLOSSARY

**Bat printing**: a form of printing in which a gelatine pad is used to transfer the image from an engraved copper plate to a ceramic surface. Unlike paper transfers, however, no printing press is needed to transfer the image from the copper plate to the gelatine pad as this can be effected by simple hand pressure.

**Bianco-sopara-bianco**: an Italian term meaning 'white-on-white'. It is a technique of painting a pure white decorative border on a slightly bluish tin glaze, producing a subtle effect. It is found only on English delftware tiles.

**Cobalt**: a metal oxide from which a blue colour is obtained. This is the principal colour in the decoration of delftware tiles because it can withstand the fierce heat of the kiln. It is dark grey in its unfired state but during the firing process it turns into a vibrant blue.

**Enamel colours**: pigments based on metal oxides used for painting or printing on an already fired glazed surface by means of a low-temperature firing (600–800°C) in a muffle kiln.

**In-glaze**: the defining characteristic of decorated tin-glazed pottery and tiles. The blue or other colour that is painted on the unfired tin glaze sinks into the glaze during the firing, fusing permanently with it.

**Kwaart**: a Dutch word derived from the Italian word *coperta*, meaning 'to cover'. It is a technique that consists of adding an extra coat of transparent glaze to decorated tin glaze, which when fired helps to create a brilliant and glossy surface.

**Maiolica**: the origins of the word are obscure but it may have come from the Spanish town of Malaga, where much tin-glazed pottery was produced in the fifteenth century, or the island of Majorca, which at that time was a major trading centre for tin-glazed pottery. The term may also be linked to an Italian Genoese trading family called Majolo. In the history of delftware tiles the term relates to tiles of the sixteenth and early seventeenth centuries painted in blue, orange, yellow and green, and which show the influence of Italian maiolica pottery.

**Manganese**: a metal whose oxide is used to produce the colour purple. After cobalt blue, it is the most common colour on Dutch tiles.

**Muffle kiln**: a kiln with an interior totally enclosed and shielded from the flames of the kiln, allowing only the heat to enter. It is used for glaze firings as well as fixing enamel colours to glazed surfaces.

**Nail holes**: indentations in two or more corners of a delftware tile caused by the protruding copper nails in the corners of a square wooden template. The nails prevent the clay from slipping when the tilemaker rotates the template while trimming the tile. Until the mid nineteenth century nail holes were a characteristic of most Dutch delftware tiles, but they are less common on English delftware tiles.

**On-glaze**: a decoration executed with enamel colours on the surface of an already fired glaze.

**Powder ground**: a closely dotted or spotted ground achieved by placing a stencil on the tile, masking the areas that are to remain white. A knife blade is drawn across the bristles of a stiff brush dipped in blue or purple pigment, causing the pigment to 'spray' on to the tile. It is a technique mainly used for decorative borders.

**Reserving**: a process in which the background is painted with a dark blue colour, leaving the design itself white. This is also known as painting 'in negative', in contrast to 'positive', where the design itself is painted directly. In the history of Dutch tiles, reserving is seen in the large corner motifs of tiles of the late sixteenth and early seventeenth centuries.

**Spons**: a Dutch word for a pricked transfer paper. A square piece of paper the size of the tile has the outlines of the design pricked through it. When placed on a tile, it allows charcoal to be pounded through the holes, leaving an impression as a guide for the painter.

**Tin glaze**: a glassy lead glaze to which tin oxide has been added, producing an opaque white glaze. The amount of tin oxide is a critical factor in determining the whiteness of the glaze.

**Transfer printing**: the transfer of a printed image from a woodcut or an engraved copper plate to a tile by means of a paper transfer tissue or a gelatine pad. The latter technique, known as bat printing, was used by the printers Sadler and Green in Liverpool to decorate plain white, but already glazed delftware tiles.

**Trek**: a Dutch word meaning 'drawing', which, in the decoration of delftware tiles, refers to the painting of the outline of the design with a fine brush, prior to adding tints and shades.

# FURTHER READING

Archer, Michael. *Delftware*. Victoria and Albert Museum, 1997.

Britton, F. *London Delftware*. Jonathan Horne Publications, 1987.

Dam, J. D. van, and others. *Dutch Tiles*. Philadelphia Museum of Art, 1984.

Horne, J. *English Tin-Glazed Tiles*. Jonathan Horne Publications, 1989.

Jonge, C. H. de. *Dutch Tiles*. Pall Mall Press, 1971.

Lemmen, H. van. *Delftware Tiles*. Laurence King, 1997.

Lemmen, H. van, and Martens, Guido von. *Blaumalerei auf Porzellan und Karamik. Blue and White Painting on China and Ceramics*. Callwey, 2001. (Text in German and English.)

Pluis, J. *De Nederlandse Tegel: Decors en Benamingen 1570–1930. The Dutch Tile: Designs and Names 1570–1930*. Primavera Press, 1997. (Text in Dutch and English.)

Ray, A. *English Delftware Tiles*. Faber & Faber, 1973.

Ray, A. *Liverpool Printed Tiles*. Jonathan Horne Publications, 1994.

*Detail of a tile panel painted in the tin-glaze technique. It depicts a winter scene in the Dutch village of Staphorst based on a picture by the Belgian artist Henri Cassiers (1858–1944). The panel was made in the 1920s either by Tichelaar in Makkum or by Westraven in Utrecht.*

# PLACES TO VISIT

## GREAT BRITAIN

*Bristol Museum and Art Gallery*, Queen's Road, Bristol BS8 1RL. Telephone: 0117 922 3571. Website: www.bristol-city.gov.uk

*The British Museum*, Great Russell Street, London WC1B 3DG. Telephone: 020 7323 8299. Website: www.thebritishmuseum.ac.uk

*John Knox's House*, 45 High Street, The Royal Mile, Edinburgh EH1 1SR. Telephone: 0131 556 9759 or 2647.

*Museum of London*, London Wall, London EC2Y 5HN. Telephone: 0870 444 3852. Website: www.museumoflondon.org.uk

*National Museum and Art Galleries on Merseyside*, William Brown Street, Liverpool L3 8EN. Telephone: 0151 478 4399. Website: www.liverpoolmuseums.org.uk

*Victoria and Albert Museum*, Cromwell Road, South Kensington, London SW7 2RL. Telephone: 020 7942 2000. Website: www.vam.ac.uk

*The Vyne*, Sherborne St John, Basingstoke RG24 9HL. Telephone: 01256 883858 or 01256 881337 (infoline). Website: www.nationaltrust.org.uk/main/w-thevyne

## THE NETHERLANDS

*Note.* The telephone numbers given here are as they should be dialled from the United Kingdom. To call from the Netherlands dial a single zero (0) instead of 0031.

*Boymans-van Beuningen Museum*, Museum Park 18-20, Rotterdam 3015 CX. Telephone: 0031 6-4419400.

*Het Princessehof Museum*, Grote Kerkstraat 11, Leeuwarden 8911 DZ. Telephone: 0031 58-2127438. Website: www.princessehof.nl

*Lambert van Meerten House Museum*, Oude Delft 199, Delft 2611 HD. Telephone: 0031 15-2602358. Website: www.lambertvanmeerten-delft.nl

*Nederlands Openlucht Museum*, Schelmsweg 89, Arnhem 6800 AP. Telephone: 0031 900-3576111. Website: www.openluchtmuseum.nl

*Nederlands Tegelmuseum*, Eikenzoom 12, Otterlo 6731 BH. Telephone: 0031 318-591519. Website: www.nederlandstegelmuseum.nl

*Rijksmuseum*, Stadhouderskade 42, Amsterdam 1070 DN. Telephone: 0031 20-6747000. Website: www.rijksmuseum.nl

*A tile by the British delftware painter Stephen Cocker showing the moon surrounded by stars. It is part of a tile series called 'The Heavens' first made in 1991.*

# INDEX